TODD TAYLOR'S

❖ 50 ❖
MOST REQUESTED
BANJO LICKS

To access audio visit:
www.halleonard.com/mylibrary

Enter Code
4529-5013-9042-3073

ISBN 978-1-57424-353-6
SAN 683-8022

Cover by James Creative Group

Copyright © 2017 CENTERSTREAM Publishing, LLC
P.O. Box 17878 - Anaheim Hills, CA 92817

www.centerstream-usa.com | centerstrm@aol.com

Special Thanks!

The Gretsch Family
Fred & Dinah Gretsch

Joe Carducci

Joe Bonsall
The Oak Ridge Boys
The Grand Ole Opry

Mitchel Meadors
Mitchel's PlateMate
Mitchel's Tone Ring Mate
Mitchel's Archtop banjo tone rings
http://www.mitchelsplatemate.com

GHS Strings

Dave Cowels
Chris Walters

Joe Tyler
Mike Moody
Paul Hinton
Ken Marler
Jimmy Diresta

Cover Photography By
Ken Marler

Table of Contents

A Word from Todd

My love for the banjo has given me many blessings in my life. I have had the opportunity to travel around the world doing the thing I love most, sharing my music with others. The one thing that I haven't taken the time to do, before now, is answer the questions about my style of playing that many fellow banjo players from all over the world have asked: How do you do that lick? How do you get that "Free Bird" or "Stairway to Heaven" sound to work on the banjo? I would have loved to be able to sit with them and share my secrets, but of course my touring and recording schedule wouldn't allow me the time. I am very excited and happy to have been given the opportunity to do just that, share my secrets, the Todd Taylor licks, with my brother and sister banjo players by way of this amazing book. I am very proud of this project because it lets me share with you the licks and personal techniques I have spent a lifetime developing. I hope you will get as much joy from it as I have gotten putting it together for you. Keep the banjo bringing smiles to faces all over the world!!

God Bless You!

Your friend,
Todd Taylor

Composed by Todd Taylor

Lick 1

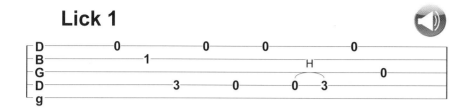

This lick is played in open G and can be repeated. I would use this lick as a intro to a song, or in the middle of a song on the turn around, for example a song like "John Hardy".

Lick 2

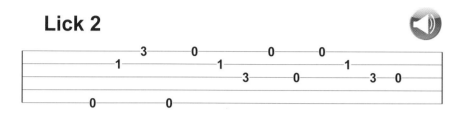

This is a lick I came up with to use as well in songs like "I'll fly Away" & "I Saw The Light" etc, it is also played in open G

Lick 3

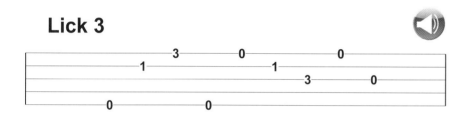

A great lick for a tag ending. I would also use this lick in a song like "Cripple Creek" as you can fit it in almost anywhere. Also played in open G.

Lick 4

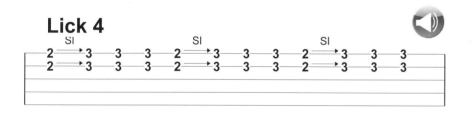

I like using this 2 note lick in a 4/4 blues tune for the intro to your break.
Play this in open G as many blues songs start on G. You would use it on the G part of the song,

Lick 5

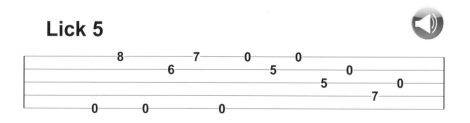

This lick can be used in songs like "Shucking The Corn" for example, you play the song one time through then use this lick to start the song the second time. It fits well in the middle of songs as well. Played in G.

Lick 6

This is a lick that I use in rock songs like my original "Todd Be Good" it is also in open G. Fits in good with many different styles of songs.

Lick 7

This is a melodic style lick in open G that can be incorporated into many songs for example songs like "Shucking The Corn", and "Dixie Breakdown".

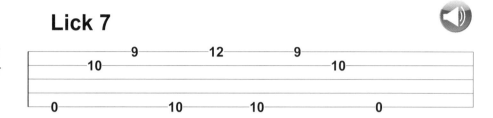

Lick 8

This is another cool lick I get many request for. I use it in many rock songs as well as "Down Yonder". Played in G

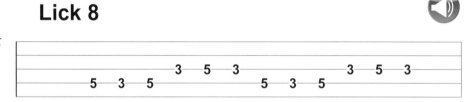

Lick 9

I use this lick in blues and rock songs. You can repeat times several times as well to form a break. Played in G.

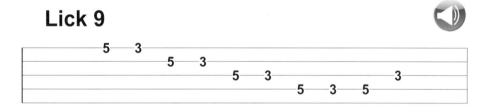

Lick 10

Another 2 note lick, I use this in blues and rock songs, even in a few bluegrass songs like "Fireball Mail".

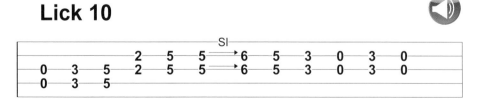

Lick 11

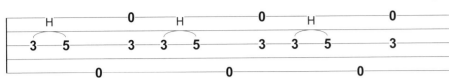

A good all around lick, I use this lick in bluegrass, rock and blues. You can throw it in on the turn around for the G portions of the songs.

Lick 12

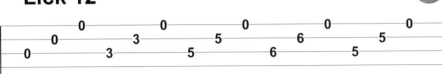

A nice 2 bar lick. For this lick I would use it in the G turn around sections of a blues song. You can also use it in some bluegrass songs as well. Give this one a try.

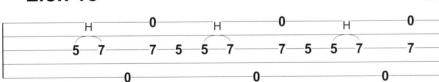

Lick 13

This lick adds some flare and its great for lots of songs: bluegrass, rock, blues as it fits in well with most songs. Example would be "Lonesome Road Blues" and "Crossroads" by Eric Clapton. Watch those hammer-on's.

Lick 14

Another all around lick, You can run this lick in just about any bluegrass song and also use it for a good ending of a song I like it for fast songs like "Shucken The Corn", "John Hardy" "Foggy Mountain Breakdown".

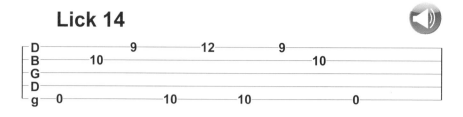

Lick 15

This lick is also more melodic and I use it in songs like "Train 45" and "Shucking The Corn".

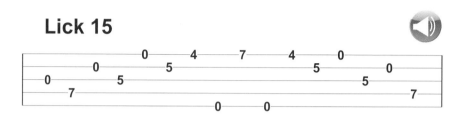

Lick 16

This is a long bluesy style lick I use in "Foggy Mountain Breakdown". Also for rock tunes and you can use it in "Clinch Mountain Back Step". Watch that hammer-on. You'll like this lick.

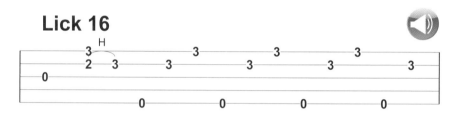

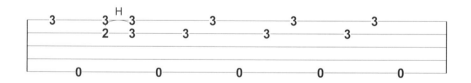

Lick 17

An all around like, you can use this lick in bluegrass, blues and rock but I use it in the slower tunes like blues tunes. Slower bluegrass tunes like "Fireball Mail". Watch out for that 5-6 slide on the 3rd string..

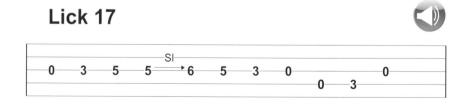

Lick 18

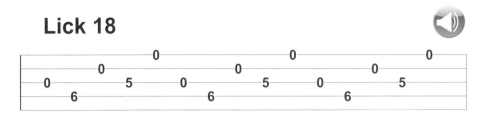

Lots of open strings here, I use this lick in songs like the popular classical guitar tune "Malaguena" and "Rhapsody For Banjo", you can also use it in bluegrass songs like "John Hardy".

Lick 19

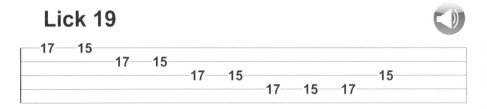

Moving high up on the neck, I use this lick in rock, blues as well on songs like "Stairway To Heaven", "Dear Old Dixie" plus my own original song "Banjo Blues".

Lick 20

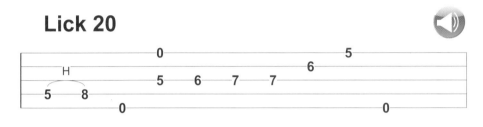

Starting right off with a hammer-on, this is a more 3 finger style lick, I use in songs for the middle parts and turn around's. Also good for songs like "I'll Fly Away" for an example.

Lick 21

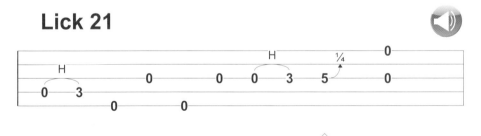

A couple of hammer-on's and a quarter tone bend on the 3rd string. This is another lick I get lots of request for. I use it in "Linus and Lucy" and "Todds Break Down".

Lick 22

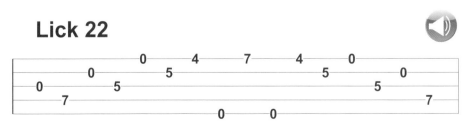

Another melodic lick I use for endings and in the middle of bluegrass songs. It will work for most all of the open G songs.

Lick 23

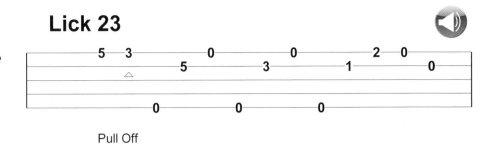

Pull Off

I use this lick in songs like "Shucking The Corn" and "Sled Ride".

Lick 24

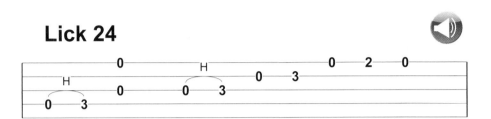

You can't go wrong with this lick. I use for beginnings and endings for many songs.

Lick 25

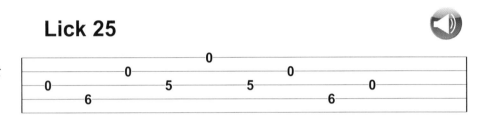

This is a lick that has a Spanish feel to it. You can even incorporate this lick in most bluegrass tunes, I like to use it in the Spanish tune "El Cancion Del Mariachi", "Lonesome Fiddle Blues" and "Back Home In Carolina"..

Lick 26

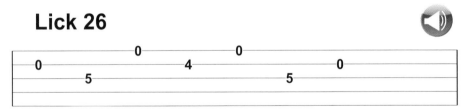

This lick can stand by itself or be added to lick #25 and used in the same manner in the same types of songs.

Lick 27

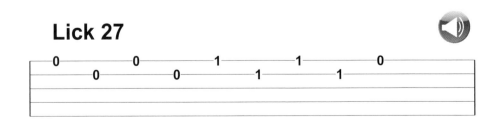

You can take this lick and use it in songs like "Dixie Breakdown", and "Spanish Grass" it works well for these songs.

Lick 28

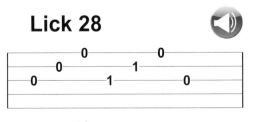

This is a variation lick that can be used in songs like "El Cumbanchero" and even blues tunes.

Lick 29

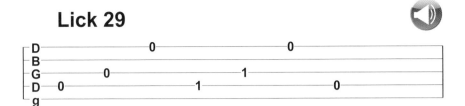

A slight variation from lick #28, use it the same way. Also sounds great putting both licks together as well.

Lick 30

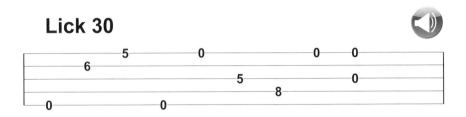

An all around lick that can be used for any song in open G. Use it to start your ending for a song, or use it anywhere in the song.

Lick 31

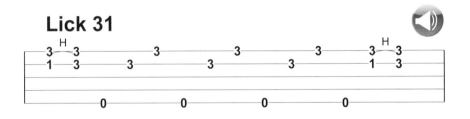

I like to use this lick on all songs bluegrass, blues and rock songs. After I start the song I use it on the turn around. Watch out for the hammer-on the start and end of the lick.

Lick 32

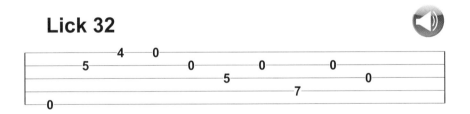

I like to use this lick in songs like "Blackberry Blossom" on the turn around. I use it every time.

Lick 33

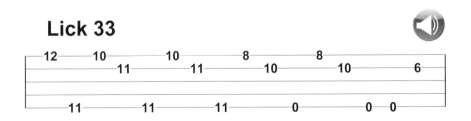

A nice long descending scale in open G that runs up the fingerboard melodic style. A good one to use in songs like "Foggy Mountain Breakdown" and "John Hardy".

Lick 34

This melodic lick is perfect for the song "Shucking The Corn" or any fast open G bluegrass song.

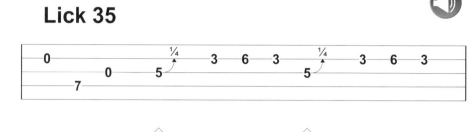

Lick 35

Here is a most requested lick I do. I use it in "Stairway To Heaven", "3-Five-n" and in most of my rock tunes. Has those 2 quarter tone bends people love. .

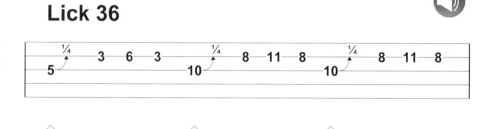

Lick 36

This 2 bar lick is also another one I use in "Free Bird". Has 3 quarter tone bends to watch out for.

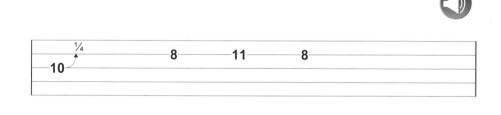

Lick 37

More quarter tone bends. I like this lick because it goes good in my song "Banjo Blues" and even the rock songs like "Free Bird".

Lick 38

Still more quarter tone bends high up on the neck. This lick is another most requested lick I get. I use it in "Free Bird" as well, and also on the blues.

Lick 39

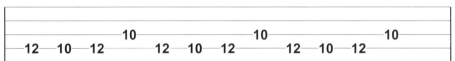

This lick is a pick up lick, you can also use in rock songs I use it in "Free Bird" and Blues

Lick 40

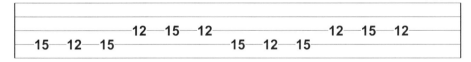

This lick is the same technique as lick 39 but moved down on the scale

Lick 41

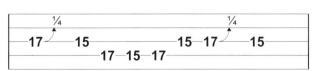

This is a good lick high up on the neck with 2 quarter tone bends. I use this one for starting a blues break or rock break. Can also be use it I the middle of songs as well.

Lick 42

Another blues lick high up on the neck. I like to use this one to start my blues song "Banjo Blues", goes well with other songs as well.

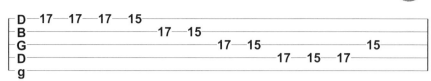

Lick 43

Play lick 42 and then this lick, notice anything different? Same lick just played in a different G position on the neck. I use this lick the same way I use lick 42.

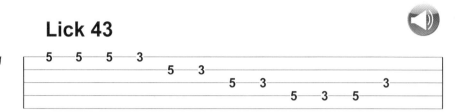

Lick 44

This lick can be used to build a break and also to end a break I use it both ways. Some nice hammer-on's on the 4th string.

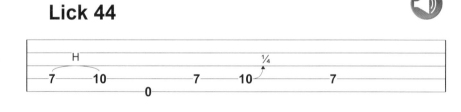

Lick 45

I also use this lick for kicking off tunes like "Train 45".

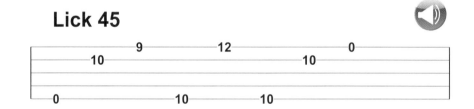

Lick 46

This lick can be used in tunes like "Theme Time" and my original song "Race Is On".

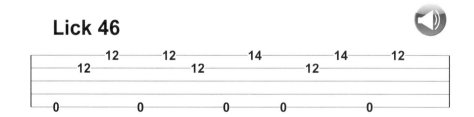

Lick 47

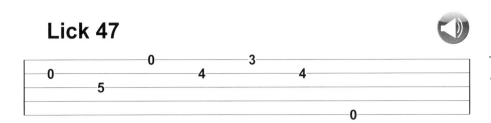

Try using use this lick in tunes like "Caravan" and "Beethoven's Fifth".

Lick 48

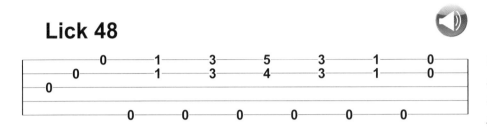

I use this in my original "Taylor's Tango" and also in "Beethoven's Fifth". Nice double notes on the first and second strings.

Lick 49

I use this in my song "Taylor's Ride" and it fits nice in many bluegrass songs like "Clinch Mountation Backstep". Couple of nice string bends too.

Lick 50

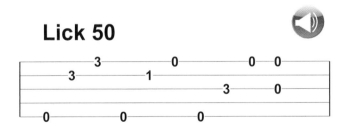

A nice lick to use in songs like "Down Yonder" etc and I also like it for "Wheel Hoss".

More Great Banjo Books from Todd Taylor...

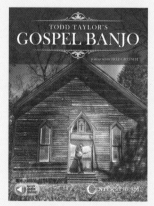